UNDERSTANDING ASIAN AMERICANS

BOOK 1 TO ASIAN IDENTITIES

BY CHEY CALISO

Introduction

Let me introduce myself, I go by Chey and I currently attend college with a major in Nutrition and Dietetics. I am a writer and I want to have a good amount of my writing having to do with the food industry.

I was born in Ohio but most of my ancestry traces back to the Philippines. The reason I'm writing this book is to have an idea about the Asian American community. This is the first ever book I will be publishing so I admit, it's not going to be as perfect.

As a disclaimer I will bring up graphic information, profanity is frequent and sexual activity will be talked about as well so I request a mature audience who can handle these sorts of subjects. It's very important for people to understand what I am talking about, so I'm going to keep it simple but include a lot of information. My goal is to be as open minded as someone can be. Obviously I'm not the most educated and I don't expect everyone to be but when someone is trying to educate you on a topic that you still chose to be close minded about on purpose then there becomes a problem.

For respect, I'm not comfortable using anyone's real names except for my acknowledgements page. Everyone else I talk about will just not be named.

When I was growing up, I learned many ignorant things from friends I had at the time, family members and even teachers. I took time to unlearn them as I got older and my whole mindset changed once I was able to think for myself. It was wrong of me to think that way and I now know better and I am even still learning to this day of topics I could be more open minded about.

When we are kids we don't understand that the

the jokes we learn from others are harmful. Children do make mistakes and they either realize it's wrong later on or they don't learn at all. From this book hopefully you can learn more about what Asian Americans go through in this country, what makes someone Asian, how the media shapes us and much more. Remember, I am not here to say we are perfect but I would like people to address and treat us like how we are humans like everyone else. Asian racism is normalized when it shouldn't be.

ASIA COUNTRIES PROFILES

North Asia: Russia

Official Language: Russian

Nationality: Russian

Currency: Ruble

Capital: Moscow

Most Common Religion: Russian Orthodox

CENTRAL ASIA

Kazakhstan

Official Language: Kazakh, Russian

Nationality: Kazakhstani

Currency: Tenge

Capital: Nur-Sultan

Most Common Religion: Islam

Kyrgyzstan

Official Language: Kyrgyz, Russian

Nationality: Kyrgyzstani

Currency: Som

Capital: Bishkek

Most Common Religion: Islam

Tajikistan

Official Language: Tajik

Nationality: Tajikistani

Currency: Somoni

Capital: Dushanbe

Most Common Religion: Islam

Turkmenistan

Official Language: Turkmen

Nationality: Turkmen

Currency: Manat

Capital: Ashgabat

Most Common Religion: Islam

Uzbekistan

Official Language: Uzbek

Nationality: Uzbek

Currency: Som

Capital: Tashkent

Most Common Religion: Islam

East Asia

China

Official Language: Mandarin

Nationality: Chinese

Currency: Renminbi

Capital: Beijing

Most Common Religion: Chinese Folk Religion

Japan

Official Language: Japanese

Nationality: Japanese

Currency: Yen

Capital: Tokyo

Most Common Religion: Shintoism

Mongolia

Official Language: Mongolian

Nationality: Mongolian

Currency: tögrög

Capital: Ulaanbaatar

Most Common Religion: Buddhism

North Korea

Official Language: Korean

Nationality: North Korean

Currency: Won

Capital: Pyongyang

South Korea

Official Language: Korean

Nationality: South Korean

Currency: Won

Capital: Seoul

Most Common Religion: Christianity

Taiwan

Official language: Mandarin

Nationality: Taiwanese

Currency: New Taiwan Dollar

Capital: Taipei

Most Common Religion: Buddhism

South Asia

Afghanistan

Official Language: Pashto, Dari

Nationality: Afghan

Currency: Afghani

Capital: Kabul

Most Common Religion: Islam

Bangladesh

Official Language: Bengali

Nationality: Bangladeshi

Currency: Taka

Capital: Dhaka

Most Common Religion: Islam

Bhutan

Official Language: Dzongkha

Nationality: Bhutanese

Currency: Ngultrum

Capital: Thimphu

Most Common Religion: Buddhism

India

Official Language: Hindi, English

Nationality: Indian

Currency: Rupee

Capital: New Delhi

Most Common Religion: Hinduism

Maldives

Official Language: Dhivehi

Nationality: Maldivian

Currency: Rufiyaa

Capital: Malé

Most Common Religion: Islam

Nepal

Official Language: Nepali

Nationality: Nepali, Nepalese

Currency: Rupee

Capital: Kathmandu

Most Common Religion: Hinduism

Pakistan

Official Language: Urdu, English

Nationality: Pakistani

Currency: Rupee

Capital: Islamabad

Most Common Religion: Islam

Sri Lanka

Official Language: Sinhala, Tamil

Nationality: Sri Lankan

Currency: Rupee

Capital: Sri Jayawardenepura Kotte, Colombo

Most Common Religion: Buddhism

South East Asia

Brunei

Official Language: Malay

Nationality: Bruneian

Currency: Brunei Dollar

Capital: Bandar Seri Begawan

Most Common Religion: Islam

Cambodia

Official Language: Khmer

Nationality: Cambodian

Currency: Riel

Capital: Phnom Penh

Most Common Religion: Buddhism

Indonesia

Official Language: Indonesian

Nationality: Indonesian

Currency: Rupiah

Capital: Jakarta

Most Common Religion: Islam

Laos

Offficial Language: Lao

Nationality: Laotian, Lao

Currency: Kip

Capital: Vientiane

Most Common Religion: Buddhism

Malaysia

Official Language: Malaysian

Nationality: Malaysian

Currency: Ringgit

Capital: Kuala Lumpur

Most Common Religion: Islam

Myanmar

Official Language: Burmese

Nationality: Burmese

Currency: Kyat

Capital: Naypyidaw

Most Common Religion: Buddhism

Philippines

Official Language: Tagalog and English

Nationality: Filipino

Currency: Pesos

Capital: Manila

Most Common Religion: Roman Catholic

Singapore

Official Language: English, Malay, Mandarin, and Tamil

Nationality: Singaporean

Currency: Singapore Dollar

Capital: Singapore

Most Common Religion: Buddhism

Thailand

Official Language: Thai

Nationality: Thai

Currency: Baht

Capital: Bangkok

Most Common Religion: Buddhism

Timor-Leste

Official Language: Portuguese and Tetun

Nationality: Timorese

Currency: United States Dollar

Capital: Dili

Most Common Religion: Roman Catholic

Vietnam

Official Language: Vietnamese

Nationality: Vietnamese

Currency: đồng

Capital: Hanoi

Most Common Religion: Vietnamese Folk Religion

West Asia

Armenia

Official Language: Armenian

Nationality: Armenian

Currency: Dram

Capital: Yerevan

Most Common Religion: Armenian Apostolic Church

Azerbaijan

Official Language: Azerbaijani

Nationality: Azerbaijani

Currency: Manat

Capital: Baku

Most Common Religion: Islam

Bahrain

Official Language: Arabic

Nationality: Bahraini

Currency: Dinar

Capital: Manama

Most Common Religion: Islam

Cyprus

Official Language: Greek and Turkish

Nationality: Cypriot

Currency: Euro

Capital: Nicosia

Most Common Religion: Greek Orthodox

Georgia

Official Language: Georgian

Nationality: Georgian

Currency: Lari

Capital: Tbilisi

Most Common Religion: Orthodox

Iran

Official Language: Farsi

Nationality: Iranian

Currency: Rial

Capital: Tehran

Most Common Religion: Islam

Iraq

Official Language: Arabic and Kurdish

Nationality: Iraqi

Currency: Dinar

Capital: Baghdad

Most Common Religion: Islam

Jordan

Official Language: Arabic

Nationality: Jordanian

Currency: Dinar

Capital: Amman

Most Common Religion: Islam

Kuwait

Official Language: Arabic

Nationality: Kuwaiti

Currency: Dinar

Capital: Kuwait City

Most Common Religion: Islam

Lebanon

Official Language: Arabic

Nationality: Lebanese

Currency: Pound

Capital: Beirut

Most Common Religion: Islam

Oman

Official Language: Arabic

Nationality: Omani

Currency: Rial

Capital: Muscat

Most Common Religion: Islam

Palestine

Official Language: Arabic

Nationality: Palestinian

Currency: Shekel

Capital: Jerusalem

Most Common Religion: Islam

Qatar

Official Language: Arabic

Nationality: Qatari

Currency: Riyal

Capital: Doha

Most Common Religion: Islam

Saudi Arabia

Official Language: Arabic

Nationality: Saudi, Saudi Arabian

Currency: Riyal

Capital: Riyadh

Most Common Religion: Islam

Syria

Official Language: Arabic

Nationality: Syrian

Currency: Pound

Capital: Damascus

Most Common Religion: Islam

Turkey

Official Language: Turkish

Nationality: Turkish

Currency: Lira

Capital: Ankara

Most Common Religion: Islam

United Arab Emirates

Official Language: Arabic

Nationality: Emirati

Currency: Dirham

Capital: Abu Dhabi

Most Common Religion: Islam

Yemen

Official Language: Arabic

Nationality: Yemeni, Yemenite

Currency: Rial

Capital: Sanaa

Most Common Religion: Islam

"PERFECT ENGLISH"

English is the Universal Language, yes but not everyone in the world speaks English. Americans complain that people who live in the US don't know how to speak English but believe it or not, English was never the official language in the United States. Since the majority spoke it that's why it was passed down to people to speak in, then it got taught in schools and spoken at public places.

It should be required for all US schools to teach a second language when we are first starting school. At least in my school we didn't start to take it until we were in sixth grade. In other countries, kids are bilingual from having to take a language course in their early school years. For me, I didn't start to take

Spanish until sixth grade, it is harder to learn a new language the older you get.

English is taught as a secondary language all around the world or people might self teach but due to a person's class status not everyone has access to know it. It might also be because of learning disabilities or that one just might not need to.

Remember that Education is a privilege. Not everyone in the world has access and if there is one thing I am grateful for, it is the education I was able to receive all these years of going to school. In a way, many of us do have privileges but we might not have all the privileges in the book. For example, the ways that I am privileged is that I have a roof over my head, access to running water, I have a toilet, electricity in my home, I was able to receive education, able-bodied, and being able to never go to bed hungry.

While it is common for people to have those privileges in the United States, there are still many countries in the world that don't have access to that kind of stuff and it may be surprising but it happens so don't make fun of people for that, even if you can help them out in any way it will make a difference in their life and yours.

In countries like India, Philippines and Singapore, English is an Official language on the side but there are people who don't speak English who are from those countries. My one grandfather did not speak English but he did speak two other languages. On the other hand, my other family members from back home or who immigrated to other countries all speak English fluently.

Countries like Thailand, Iraq and Kazakhstan, English is not as common. Of course there are people who are from those countries that speak English but the language isn't commonly spoken like how it is in the other countries.

Please do not come up to a person who isn't

white and "compliment" them on how "good" they can speak English. It's actually rude and weird. It makes people believe that just because they have ancestry that isn't from Europe or that they were born in a country besides the United States that everyone speaks "broken" English. There's no such thing as "perfect English", we all have different levels of speaking a language.

One thing I will never understand is why do Americans get so angry when they hear someone speaking another language? Why do they want to eavesdrop so bad? Do they not realize that some non-native English speakers are more comfortable speaking in their native tongue?

If you are the type of person to think the only reason someone is speaking in another language is because they are talking shit then you need to realize the world doesn't revolve around you. People who do speak another language are usually just having a casual conversation with the other person and they aren't even thinking about you. Sorry to tell you, but you're not special.

Why can't people mind their business? It's not rude to speak in another language, especially when the person is talking to someone else who can communicate with them. If you care so much then how about you learn another language? I know many people like to make fun of the way someone speaks just because they are from another country or speak another language but let's be real, the people who mainly do that can't even speak another language themselves.

I feel bad for the kids who are afraid to speak their native language in front of their English speaking friends. I feel even worse when the parents are upset that the kids feel that way. With the way society judges us we can't have anything in life. We are judged for anything, basically we are judged by how we live our life.

There's some people who grow up regretting not knowing their native language and a reason why they didn't want to learn it was because kids wanted to grow up "normal" like their peers. Why did kids feel that way? It's just a language. But if you think about it, being bilingual opens a lot of doors for you. Better chances at jobs, traveling opportunities, and it expands your brain activity. Sadly, kids don't know much about life yet, they take it for granted and don't realize until it's too late that they had an opportunity.

Why I'm Not Bilingual

As a child, my mom attempted to teach me words in the two other languages she speaks but it never worked out for me. Due to my parents working all the time, I was always with my aunt and she only cared about wanting me to speak "good English" because if I didn't, according to her, then people would make fun of me. When I was learning how to talk she would get frustrated with my grammatically incorrect speaking so I was ashamed to talk in general. She blamed part of the reason I talked like that on my mom but in reality it wasn't even my mom's fault for how I used English sentences, it's common for children to mess up like that. This is why we take a class in school called English.

When you're a child, you don't think about it but once you grow up you realize how much it affected you. I regret growing up not being able to speak my native languages and now my aunt wishes I spoke Tagalog as well. Once I got older I did want to learn another language but the older you are, the harder it is to learn. I am learning Spanish right now and have used multiple resources to be able to learn it. It will take me a while to become a conversational speaker in the language.

CULTURAL APPROPRIATION

Cultural Appropriation is when you take an object from a specific culture (sometimes religion) while using it as an aesthetic without knowing or caring about the cultural significance it holds. For me, the reason I hate when people appropriate culture is because sometimes we were made fun of for practicing these customs or wearing these certain types of clothing coming from our culture when we were growing up but then later on, people from other communities will act like they started it and now it's considered cool and trendy when they do it themselves.

In this section, some of these items that I talk about are from religions, which I will include here if

the religion happens to originate in Asia. I will be
talking about the origins and how people appropriated
this specific item.

Appropriation in Asian cultures:

<u>Bindi</u> - Girls who go to Coachella like to wear Bindis
during that day but have no idea what the significance
of wearing them is. So let me tell you, bindis first
originated in the Hindu religion. Hinduism originated
in the Indian subcontinent. Red bindis are most
common for married women. It can also be considered
as the third eye, to keep bad luck away.
During 1987, a hate group called "The Dotbusters"
was located in Jersey City, New Jersey. They were
known to brutally attack South Asian people,
specifically wanting to target Hindus.

<u>Fox Eye Trend</u> - Some people will say that Asians are
overreacting but we aren't. It's literally our eyes

being made fun of for so long now it's trendy when other girls are able to do it then stop right when they take their hands off their face, so yeah we are annoyed. Plus, the pose wasn't even that cute.

<u>Hijab -</u> A head covering that many women from the Muslim community prefer to wear around men outside of the family. For some muslim women to feel even more modest, they might also prefer to wear a Chador, Niqab, or a Burka. Not all women in the Muslim faith prefer to wear coverings so they don't have to, but when you enter a mosque you are required to wear a hijab, then wear loose fitting clothing with skin being covered as much as possible.

For some reason, people think Coachella is the time to dress up like other people's cultures for the day. You see people from outside communities wearing Hijabs, Dashikis, cornrows, Bindis, headdresses, kimonos etc. just to attend some music festival. I understand that

Coachella is a place to have fun but do it respectfully. People are bothered with non-muslims wearing the hijab because muslim women have been attacked for so long especially when they wear their religious attire. There have been known incidents where people have ripped off the hijabs of Muslim women and even one story known that a man went up to a pregnant hijabi woman and kicked her stomach resulting in losing her baby.

Kimono - Kimonos originated from Japan. They are usually worn for weddings, tea ceremonies, formal and traditional events, and funerals. Depending on age and marital status, the color of the Kimono varies. Men's kimonos are usually made of matte fabrics while womens are usually made from silk.

One fashion company has been accused of cultural appropriation by selling kimonos worn by people who are not of Japanese descent. They listed it as a costume that consisted of hair sticks, kimono and an obi (used like a belt to keep the robe together). The outfit is shown to be sexualized which offended people especially from that culture. As of this time, the outfit is no longer on the website.

<u>Qipao</u> - Also known as cheongsam, originated in China. Today you might see them look tight fitting and in the color red. In the 1920s, it was used by Chinese women to bring empowerment and to show off their beauty as The Qing dynasty displayed oppression towards women. They expected women to stay in the house so they could do house work and look after the children and bind their feet. One way for Chinese women to protest was to take what the cheongsam originally was and change it into their own modern style.
On twitter, a girl posted herself wearing the Qipao as a prom dress. The other photos show her and her

friends doing stereotypical poses which sparked outrage. She wanted to say that she was "appreciating" the culture because of how much she claims to love Chinese culture. It is clear she wanted to mock people by the poses they did afterwards.

In certain stores, they sold the Qipao without giving the true meaning to it and even on one store's website, they even included the term "oriental" while trying to sell it.

<u>Sacred Temple</u> - A Buddhist place of worship is a temple. Countries with Buddhism as the predominant religion are Thailand, Taiwan, Myanmar, Cambodia, Bhutan, Sri Lanka, Laos, Singapore and Mongolia. The Buddha originally came from Lumbini, Nepal. His real name was Siddhartha Gautama and is not considered a God. He grew up wealthy but was not blind to noticing poverty in the world so he gave up the luxurious lifestyle and decided to spend the rest of

his time teaching his beliefs and many eventually became followers.

A rapper had a music video out but later deleted the video due to the harassment coming from viewers. The women who dressed up in traditional Asian clothing and danced in front of a Buddhist temple were also called out for it. Many people were mad because of this. The rapper recalled he was approved with the leader and owner of the location but the person whose father is the president of the temple exposed the rapper saying he allowed him to film a video but he would have to see the video before posting which the president never got to see the video until his daughter showed him, then he said he would never approve something like that.

Turban - Many men who practice the Sikh faith never cut their hair as they look at it as sacred. The hair is part of God's creation so it should not be changed in an unnatural form. The turbans are worn to protect their hair.

A rich clothing company has been known to profit from using the Turbans in fashion shows and sell a Turban for $790.00. The problem with this is that the Turban is not an accessory non-Sikhs use in their fashion, it has religious significance that belongs to the group of Sikh men. An actor from a children's show has also called out the company for modeling it off in their fashion show.

There have been stories of Sikh men wanting to cut their hair off to avoid harassment in the public. So yeah, it is reasonable to bash this company for selling turbans as accessories that are now found considered "trendy" by people who aren't from that community.

Culture is not a costume! Some traditional outfits are not worn once in a while but sometimes a daily wear like a hijab. There's ignorant people who go to Coachella once a year to wear a hijab when they know nothing about Islam. There's stories of former hijabi girls who stop wearing their hijabs due to bullying and physical torment. I understand many things from someone else's culture are beautiful, culture is beautiful but these objects have cultural significance and should not be worn by you if you are not from the culture.

Racism At My Highschool

I dread writing this part as I do not like looking back on highschool. My principal during my Freshman and Sophomore year of being there did not tolerate it and handled it well. A lot of the staff didn't tolerate it, it was mainly the students.

The stuff I went through wasn't major compared to other horror stories I've heard but with my experiences I would just feel dehumanized which is a really crummy feeling especially since I am sensitive.

<u>Racism taking place at my highschool:</u>

1. In my Freshman year, I was literally called a cat eater by over seven different people. Literally my third day there, this kid asked "How many cats do you eat in a

week?" and that's when I knew I was always going to hate high school. He would also say the n-word and would mock Asian accents to me. When my friend at the time found out he then told him how bothered I was and the guy decided to apologize so I acted like I forgave him but in reality I couldn't.

2. This was probably the kid I hated the most. I knew so much tea about him and wanted to call him out in front of the whole class but I couldn't get myself to do it because I wanted to be the bigger person to everyone and now I do regret not exposing him in high school because this kid would say that I eat cats and even called me a C**nk. He was also so rude to me for no reason but was so nice to everyone else. He started to act nice in my senior year although I knew he was still talking shit about me behind my back so that's why in workout class I took a workout band and stretched it back all the way to where it flung in his face. I pretended like it was an accident to the

teacher even though the student knew it was fully intentional when I turned around laughing with my friend. Doing that made up for all those years he would be mean to me.

3. In Junior year I went to a football game to meet up with my friends. While we were on our phones and messing around, I overheard some lady talking about doing nails at the salon. Then I paid more attention and heard her say "I do for you, hey I do for you, you will have nice nail" in a fake Asian accent. Since her daughter who went to my school as well joined in, I hated whenever she would talk to me so I would ignore her. When I went to Marshall's one day, I ran into them and right before I left, I walked past them and I might've said "putang ina mo." Please do not translate that.

4. I knew a guy in my high school with an Asian fetish and went to homecoming with the other Asian girl in my grade. The problem with that was when he was

talking about her to his friends, he made a comment saying "I bet that pussy is tighter than her eyes." Then in Junior year, he told me "You know America had the Philippines for a while so we were able to do anything we wanted to you guys."

5. Through a mutual friend, I became friends with this girl by the end of Freshman year. Together we would do volunteer work in the elementary school during the first quarter of Sophomore year. The racism part of her didn't jump out until Junior year.

When we were Juniors she dated this guy and they would both call me "illegal immigrants" and would say I would get deported if I didn't like a certain thing. They knew I was born in The United States but made jokes like that because apparently deportation and immigrant jokes are part of their sense of humor. Once her and her boyfriend broke up she went to me for moral support. I actually did feel bad until she started to make fun of his new girlfriend and even said "she has ugly Asian eyes."

6. I knew someone in school whose family member hated this one kid a grade below me all because he was Vietnamese. The reason he hated him was because his family member was killed in the Vietnam war. After hearing that all I could do was question the man's ignorance because I'm pretty sure whoever killed his family member was not related to the student, you just look for an excuse to hate them.

7. During Senior year, this person I used to be friends with in Freshman year said "Chinese and African people are unsanitary." He talked about how he hated Chinese people because "They had Corona." This guy was the type of person to joke about people's insecurities thinking it was funny but honestly it sounded stupid and I don't understand why people liked him. We had to stop being friends in Sophomore year because of "differences."

8. Here is the worst one, my Junior and Senior year

teacher. He told us how he would mimic the Chinese accent and that he doesn't do it anymore because "he can't get the tone right." Students found him funny when he said "Hey, don't be a woman in Saudi Arabia if you get caught driving you will die!" and the time he heard a negative story about a pilot who happened to be Japanese so he proceeded to say "I would not be riding in a plane if the pilot is Japanese."

As much as people tried to get me to hate myself for being POC, I couldn't do it. I loved where I came from. Even though people made fun of me for being "different" there were a lot of cool and amazing things coming from my culture. When I took a vacation to the Philippines when I was fifteen, they were all nice to me and even though I would have been considered "different" they didn't make me feel that way. They always made me feel so welcomed.

RACISM USED IN THE ENTERTAINMENT INDUSTRY

I honestly cannot think of a Celebrity that I am a fan of. I have no desire to know what celebrities are doing daily. Anything I know about celebrities today is from memes on instagram. I have concluded that celebrities do not care about being "cancelled" and only apologize because they got caught. They still will continue to have those thoughts and be problematic.

As a kid I used to look up to a lot of celebrities, even be obsessed with a handful of them as that's what many people my age did back then. Once I got older, around high school and did a little of "finding myself" I realized that I shouldn't be looking up to celebrities. Yeah they were good for listening to music and watching them on tv but who is responsible for you as a person? You are. They aren't here to raise you or your kids, they are there strictly for entertainment purposes.

People showing signs of racism/xenophobia to the Asian Community:

<u>Resurfaced Tweets:</u> This actor had tweeted these at a young age. Once the movie he starred in rose to popularity for the remarkable representation for the Asian community, the tweets of him resurfaced. After the 2011 Earthquake and Tsunami that happened in Japan, his tweets read "Dogs can sense earthquakes. Too bad Japan ate them all."

<u>Library Rant:</u> All the sources I have gotten from this are said to have happened in 2011. A young woman who attended UCLA posted a video online complaining about how "Asian people are always noisy", mocking our languages and how we don't have "American manners." She then gets annoyed with Asian family

members always getting together.

<u>Changing a last name to get better roles in Hollywood:</u> The actress expresses how proud she is to be half Chinese to the media but due to Hollywood's shade they preferred her name to sound rather American than hearing her original name. For the respect she has for her Chinese father, she agreed to use her father's American sounding first name. She has shown that she had been unhappy from the name change as she adores her background. She has mentioned that she can speak Mandarin, takes part in Chinese culture and has even lived in China for a period of time.

<u>Rappers using a racial slur in their song:</u> I can't even lie, they have some great beats to their songs but the slurs they included were unnecessary. In the lyrics you can hear them saying the word "C**nks." Not even did he just offend a group of people but one from the group also dated a rapper who was part Chinese.

<u>Comedy skits on Vietnamese Nail Technicians:</u> People like to get manicures and pedicures done but once they walk out of the door they then start mocking the worker's accents. There's so many comedy skits based on mocking nail technicians' accents and not even that but it's just so childish at this point. Like I don't know about everyone else but I don't find making fun of people's accents funny and most of the people making fun of accents can't even speak another language.

The reason that so many nail technicians happen to be Vietnamese is because refugees came to the United States when the Vietnam war was happening. These women were left with almost nothing. They didn't understand much English but were granted a solution of opening nail salons as it didn't require as much communication.

An actress started to show off her nails in movies she starred in. She gave these Vietnamese women the opportunity to keep practicing by letting them go to beauty school to educate them on nails.

<u>Former Musical.ly star's Xenophobia:</u> She goes on instagram live saying "I'm sorry not trying to be racist or anything but everytime I see a Chinese person I go ... don't breathe. He says it's the Chinese virus. I mean it came from China, so it's the Chinese virus." Does this girl not realize that she got famous by an app made by Chinese people? Since Musical.ly technically doesn't exist anymore she is now known as a singer. Anyways, shortly after she issues an apology, you can clearly tell that she is forced to apologize because of the loads of hate she is getting then defending herself that she is human and that we all make mistakes. I think she's at that age where you know what you meant to say and now you just can't handle the amount of hate you're getting from it. So in that case, learn your mistake and issue a real apology to the community you affected because I know that all of the other people who forgave you are not from that community that has been affected. So what do their opinions mean in that situation? Irrelevance.

<u>Known celebrity's disrespect towards the Asian community</u>: So there is a celebrity who is known as a writer and actress for popular films. She always makes jokes about Vietnamese people and oversexualizes the women from Asian communities in her films. It's almost like it's what makes up her personality trait because of how much she puts it in her films and talks about it so much.

I have mixed feelings about cancel culture. Yeah I do think cancel culture is toxic but other times, it gives a redemption for someone famous but what I notice is that many celebrities do not care about cancel culture and it's probably because they already have a bunch of fans that in the end there will still be many people there for them no matter how problematic they might get. I'm sure there are celebrities out there who are truly sorry for their mistakes and if they learn their lesson and have apologized to the community they affected in the right way, then there will be people from that community who are going to forgive.

Racial slurs

Ling Ling - This really isn't a slur but many of us do get offended by it. People use it to make fun of people with traditional Asian names. It's mainly directed towards Asian people in East Asia and other surrounding parts like Southeast Asia.

C**nk - This term was first used around the 20th century. The term was mainly directed towards people of Chinese descent as many white people in America saw them as a threat and did not like them due to the white people believing that the Chinese people affected their living standards.

G**k - Insulting term used for Asian people. A lot of

times directed to ethnic groups in East or Southeast Asia.

J*p - Directed towards people of Japanese descent. Before WWII in the United States, it wasn't seen as derogatory as it was just used as a shortened version of the word Japanese. After WWII, people decided to use it in a degrading way which is why people shouldn't say the word.

P*ki - Term directed towards people of Pakistani descent. You would more than likely hear this term in The UK. It was first used in 1964 when the rise of South Asian immigration came to The United Kingdom and people used it in a derogatory way.

Yellowface & Brownface

Yellowface is when you dress up as an East Asian person giving off a harmful representation. Non-Asian people tend to change up their eyes, face and sometimes teeth (coming from a stereotype that East Asians have buck teeth) and use it for a character on a tv show, movie or a skit for a youtube video.

Blackface, Brownface, Yellowface, and Redface are offensive because the only intentions of what people want to do to these characters are to make fun of them. People see nothing wrong with this and don't realize it is dehumanizing to a group of people yet we are called sensitive because we would like to be seen as human beings and not someone as less than another person but that's something they won't understand.

Yellowface was introduced as early as the early 1900s and it is still being portrayed today in the twenty-first century. It is said that Yellowface existed due to white actors making Hollywood movies better if the white people were in them instead of actual Asian people. This shows that the audience wanted to see us as entertainment instead of people they had respect for. If you look at all of the movies and shows involving Yellowface or any type of that matter, you can see that all of it is mockery, everything in it is just to insult and put someone down.

As the number of Asians increases in the United States, there are still some directors that will still cast other people rather than the person who would fit perfectly into the role. You hear about white actors whitewashing films all the time.

Brownface is commonly known as someone who dresses up as a stereotypical South Asian, Southeast Asian, Latinx or Hispanic, Pacific

Islander or an Arab person to portray negative stereotypes of people in those communities.

Stop Using the Term "illegal immigrant"

If you happen to use the term "illegal immigrant" or "illegal alien" then it's probably best to get it out of your vocabulary right now. Why are you calling human beings different nationalities from you aliens in the first place? They are clearly human who have every right to do what they want in their life.

"But these immigrants steal our jobs!" No they don't. It's pretty easy to get a job in The United States if you look in the right places. The internet is a helpful source to find jobs plus companies offer people jobs all the time.

No human being is "illegal" especially on stolen land by you know who. Why should there be a limit to where people can move to or visit? Not that it's any of our business on the resident status of other people but undocumented immigrant is the correct term if one happens to not have records of residency in the place they currently happen to live in.

MODEL MINORITY

The meaning of model minority is used mainly towards Asian-Americans to classify us that we are on a higher level of privilege as compared to other minority groups. Every minority group has been oppressed and it's not a competition. We are currently dealing with a lot in our community, so no, the model minority doesn't exist.

The latest issue in the Asian American community is the skyrocketing hate crimes. When the incident of the Georgia killing six Asian women happened, then that's when people started to pretend they care about Asian people. This isn't some temporary trend, we are humans like everyone else. This whole hate crime situation towards Asian Americans proves that we are not a model minority. Even with the normalized jokes made towards us, it makes me feel personally that we aren't looked at as human beings.

FETISHIZATION

Another big problem we have in our community is being the victim of racial fetishization. Many think it's harmless to have racial fetishes but it's actually gross and believe it or not, people will go out of their way to get their fetish to fulfill themselves. Exactly like when Western men go to Asia for sex tourism.

Why racial fetishes are wrong:
The way a relationship works if you connect with a person. If you only like them for their looks and/or sex then it just won't work out. You need to at least have some things in common and you need to love their personality.
There is a huge difference between love and lust in a relationship. Don't get me wrong, it's totally okay to

go for looks over personality first but if you really want to work out with them, then get to know what they like, things you have in common and if in your opinion think they have a great personality.

Example: If you choose a woman just because she is Asian and don't care to know how she is as a person and/or believing these stereotypes about her then that is a fetish. You chose an Asian woman because you believe she can be this image you might think of her but in reality it might be way different from what you expect.

Don't just choose a person because of their race. You can date whatever race you want but don't be opposed to dating another race because they are this race that you don't really prefer. If you find them attractive, fits your standards, you love their personality etc. then why should their race matter?

I would not like to be fetishized because I want some-one to see me more than my looks. I think someone should like me for my personality and my interests. I think there are many great qualities about me and if you like my physical appearance then it should be counted as a plus.

When people fetishize Asians, they sometimes refer to it as "Yellow Fever" which it's not only wrong to say you have a fever for us but calling us yellow is offensive as well. The term "yellow" to describe Asian people (mainly directed towards East Asian) and was first used by the Europeans hundreds of years ago. They cared so much about not wanting to associate with people like them so they decided to call them "yellow" while in reality the Asians they were referring to were the same skin tone as them.

As Asian women, we are extremely sexualized along with articles of clothing that come from our countries. For example, the qipao and Japanese school girl outfits. Even some Asian women have mentioned through tiktok that they would get compared to one of the most famous former adult film actresses just because they wore glasses in school. Which nothing against that adult film actress but these girls that have said that aren't comfortable being looked at sexually by different people. Everything is literally so sexualized at this point especially when you wear glasses but glasses are literally an object for someone to see better.

Sex work is a dangerous job where many people are taken advantage of everywhere in the world. Many people who aren't sex workers think it's so easy yet there is a dark side to these types of jobs and not only that but many people who aren't sex workers will believe it is not work at all.

Sex tourism in Asia is a huge problem while it is also common. Prostitution is illegal in many countries but people still do it to support their family members or there are people especially as a minor who are trafficked into sexual slavery who cannot consent to the acts given to them. Many older men like to travel, but many of them like to travel for the sole purposes of taking advantage of young people and to satisfy their needs with their Asian fetish as implied by many men being interviewed for news articles.

In Thailand, prostitution is illegal yet there are many prostitutes out there. In 2019, it was said that around twenty four thousand people were arrested for this act. In this case, consenting prostitutes in Thailand do it because of the amount of money they get paid.

DATING

Personally I think it is hard to date if you're an Asian woman when you date outside your race. I know many Asian people who date outside their race and that is okay but it's important that you're being respected along with your partner. Everytime it happened to me I was either fetishized, they mocked my culture or both but in reality, before I was eighteen I didn't choose the men they chose me and I agreed to go out with them to see if they offered something good but it never worked out for me which is why I made a standards list of more than one-hundred requirements and I did the choosing.

For all interracial and intercultural relationships, when you date that person, you're going to need to learn about their culture and respect the cultural differences they might have.

One time, I met some guy, I wasn't looking for anything serious but I just wanted to look around. We then went onto snapchat and talked about ourselves, so everything was going smoothly, until he posted on his story of his friend mocking asian accents while eating his Asian food while the guy I met with was laughing in the background. He then has the audacity to get pissed off at me for unadding him on snapchat.

Another time I met this one guy, (it also wasn't serious) he snapchats me saying "I see the Philippines flag in your bio, you're not going to stab me are you?" so I say "no why would I stab you?" and he replies "my friends have dated Filipina women and they were crazy." Like this bitch didn't even know my last name and already assuming I'm like a few girls his homeboys have dated, I have many Filipino friends who would never hurt anyone.

Those were probably the two worst experiences

that had to do with my race and men I was looking around with, which honestly in someone else's perspective it's not a big deal because people have been through worse but it was just something that really annoyed me.

In the past I've seen youtube videos called "What race wouldn't you date and why?" and confidently many people said they would not date an Asian person, the main reasons are because of believing the stereotypes of us eating dogs and that we can't see.

I guarantee you every race has attractive people, if you have never seen an attractive person from a certain race or ethnic background then the problem is you and the stereotypes of that group of people control your mind. There are over seven billion people in this world coming from all different backgrounds and some of people will refuse to date a certain race because they believe in the stereotypes about them and/or think they all look the same.

COLONIZATION

Influences from colonization today:

Cambodia from France:

Architecture: There are still buildings today with French architecture.

Food: Baguettes are common to eat in Cambodia.

Lebanon from France:

Language: While Arabic is the official language of Lebanon, it is also common for people to know English and French as well. In some instances, many know French from colonial rule and it was passed down ever since.

Philippines from Spain:

Language: Some words that are both Spanish and Tagalog: Route (Ruta) and age (edad). There are many other words that have the same pronunciation but have different spellings to it.

Religion: The majority of The Philippines is Catholic which was brought from Spain as early as the 1500s.

Surnames: Common surnames of Filipinos may include Santos, Cruz, Navarro, or Torres. One of the main reasons we have Spanish surnames is because the Governor general during 1849, wanted Filipinos to adopt Spanish surnames so census counting would be easier for the Spaniards.

Over half the countries in Asia have been colonized, mainly from Europe. Colonialism has impacted the world in numerous different ways. Two include when the colonizers brought diseases into the new countries they invaded and created new laws that contravened the native people's culture. Although many think colonialism had great impacts, it was mostly negative through the Native people's side.

Coronavirus

During the start of Covid, I was a senior in High school. When I first heard on the news about Covid-19, the first thing I predicted was the rise of hate crimes and xenophobia towards Asian people. I didn't want to think more negatively than what was already happening but I was thinking about reality.

All through the media I saw foolish jokes that destroyed our image even more as Asian people. They called us bat eaters, threatened to hurt and kill us and even physically assaulted our people when they got the chance, this family even killed this one girl's cat. This was all because the virus happened to originate in China so due to the location it came from, we were all responsible for something we couldn't control.

Because of this, a movement called Stop Asian Hate was created to end the hate crimes happening towards the Asian community. It was to protest to stop the ongoing violence happening towards the Asian community.

WE CREATED YOUR NECESSITIES AND ITEMS YOU REFUSE TO LIVE WITHOUT

Many people make sure to bash the Asian community yet drive cars that were from South Korea, buy anime merchandise even though anime started in Japan, and eat our cultural foods. People love to wear clothes that have an East Asian alphabet on it yet say "Ching chong ching" when they hear that East Asian person with an accent. So you don't like us, but have to rely on us for our inventions?

Some Items that originated in Asia:

<u>China</u> - Candles, silk, toothbrush, kites

<u>Japan</u> - Anime, Karaoke

India - Chess, shampoo

Iraq - Soap

Timeline of What Happened to Asians During US History

<u>The Chinese Exclusion Act (1882):</u> The purpose of this was not to allow Chinese people to come into the country and work. The 21st US president officially signed this into a law on May 6, 1882. This became very effective as the Chinese population happening in the United States dramatically decreased as they couldn't get in the United States along with violence being struck towards them which in some cases led to death.

This was meant to only last for ten years but then extended it for ten more years in 1892 by the Geary Act and then the law changed and was made permanent in 1902 by the same law. Many Chinese people wanted to work in America so they could support their families back home.

Although they considered the act repealed in 1943 during World War II when China and The United States were allies, it still didn't allow as many Chinese immigrants to come into The US until the Immigration Act of 1965.

<u>Japanese Internment Camps (1942):</u> During World War II, Japanese people were rounded up and sent to internment camps because of the attack on pearl harbor that happened on December 7, 1941.

Since the country Japan was a US enemy at the time, they decided to not only put in Japanese people from Japan but also Japanese people born in America as well. Issei was someone from Japan while a nisei was someone born in the US in this case, and had parents from Japan.

From 1942 to the end of 1945 it was required by the US government that Japanese people needed to stay in these camps all because of paranoia with other Americans. The last internment camp closed in March of 1946 located in Tule Lake, California. They could only bring what they carried with them, the rest of their belongings, property and businesses no longer existed once they came back home. The Civil Liberties act of 1988 was to send out an apology to the Japanese people and give only $20,000 to the surviving Japanese people who were in the camp.

Dotbusters (1987):

A hate group that is said to want to threaten and attack Indian people, they got their name from Hindu women who wear bindis on their forehead. This took place in New Jersey and was most prevalent in 1987. This hate group was responsible for many attacks, especially with a victim they beat into a coma and he died four days after, yet this was not proven a hate crime when it came to the court case.

DROP YOUR RACIST FRIENDS

Your peers probably have the biggest effect on you so dropping the racist friends you associate with is for your own good. If you keep letting what your "friends" say to you slide then it's just going to make them feel stronger. If you're in that situation then you don't realize how bad it is now but once you get out of it you realize how terrible it was to be friends with them.

In high school, I can't believe I let it slide too much. It made me feel like the weaker person. The thing was, I felt like I couldn't make new friends. The high school I went to had around three hundred forty students, everyone knew everyone and knowing how I was and what people were like in that school I wasn't comfortable branching out to new people. In high school, I felt like I was forced to have these friends due to the small population of that school and that we were in the same classes so I had to talk to them each day. Fortunately, outside of school I had many friends of different cultures and they didn't make me feel less of a person the way my high school friends did.

In the end, I chose a college that barely anyone from my high school went to. I was able to meet a lot more people like me and didn't feel as left out like I did in high school. At my University we have representation for all different groups which helps everyone feel included.

What I learned about having these racist friends is that they want to use you as the token POC friend. They think since you're their token that it's okay to make these assumptions and stereotype people like you.

You can always try to educate them, it's worth a

shot but you don't have to do that. It's not your job to teach them, they should know. If they end up continuing those negative beliefs then drop them. You don't need to hang out with people who will try to hurt your feelings.

WE NEED TO ACCEPT EVERYONE

I had a family member that used to be close to us and she was the most close minded person I've ever known. I wasn't fond of being around her during my childhood. In eighth grade she even called me a slur. I'm not even from that group but I still was livid she called me that. It was derogatory and no matter what community I was from, I would still be offended the same way because you just don't degrade a person different from you. I never told my parents that but I would tell them I'm not very fond of her because she did stuff during childhood but my mom has a way of thinking that since she is family that I have to stay in contact. So once I was able to make decisions for myself, I dropped her.

When I was a kid she would make fun of how my physical features looked and made fun of the way my mom spoke English yet she can't even form a sentence in Tagalog and trust me I've seen her try, it made me cringe. When I was a toddler and I was starting to learn how to talk sometimes she would say "that's not the proper way of speaking, if you talk like that people are going to make fun of you.", and "let me teach you English, not your mom." She would say all this offensive stuff then get offended when someone said something about her beliefs. Overall she was emotionally abusive and I grew up thinking it was how a person older than you should treat you.

I have a lot of white people in my family and the stuff they would say about Filipinos would disgust me. They would say that Filipina women were gold diggers, hookers and would overall believe that Filipinos in general were thieves and disgusting. One even called Filipinos monkeys and "slaves of the world" (coming from the stereotype that Filipinos work as maids) but then had the audacity to deny that they were racist. Not all of them were bad and thought that way but I felt like I had a good reason to not trust any of them and to avoid them.

Americans are known to be ethnocentric. Many of them believe that America is the greatest country in the world and will think their customs are the correct way. That's clearly not how it works. When going to another country, you have to respect their laws and cultural differences. It may take time to adjust but remember, you are their guest and letting you experience their culture.

As a kid I always had an interest in learning about different cultures. I like knowing about their traditions and cultural beliefs. It's what makes the world beautiful. My views tell me to love everyone. We aren't supposed to think of ourselves as superior to anyone else, instead love everyone equally. No culture has "wrong" traditions, it's just a different way of life rather than what you're used to and in their native

countries obviously those customs are allowed

to be practiced.

WHY RACISM AND XENOPHOBIA IS DANGEROUS

Have you ever known someone who said something along the lines "I'm not racist but I make racist jokes?" It's basically in the same category of what can be considered racist. Racism can be considered calling someone racial slurs, disliking someone because they are a certain race, believing the stereotypes coming from that race, thinking your race is better than others, making jokes about that race and fetishization.

Racist jokes are so normalized and people who make racist jokes do not take actual issues seriously. They don't realize that it can lead to threats, attacks and even killing to minorities. When corona first started, people started making jokes about how Chinese people eat bats along with calling them "bat soup eaters." Part of this led to other people believing that every Asian person who looked Chinese to them had corona and attacked them for something they couldn't control.

During this covid era, many Asians are being attacked and killed, especially when we have nothing to do with the virus. It really did bring out people's true colors.

Some examples of xenophobia:

1. Telling a person to go back to their country. In some instances this can be considered racist as you are assuming a non-white person is from a different country just because they are POC.

2. One former US president's fear of Japanese people taking over put these people in dangerous positions. His xenophobia led to the imprisonment of Japanese people who had nothing to do with Pearl Harbor. He

thought that since random people who happened to be from Japan did it that he had to blame all of them and give innocent people this punishment.

3. Using derogatory comments to describe a different group of people.

4. Stereotyping certain ethnic groups

5. Refusing and/or using negative comments because of cultural differences.

6. Saying rude things about people's traditional attire.

THE DIFFERENCE BETWEEN RACE, NATIONALITY AND ETHNICITY

When people in The US asked my nationality I would just say Asian-American but in reality they more than likely are talking about ethnicity. I guess I did say that in the past just to be smart with people and didn't say anything else because it was draining to explain. I felt like people should have known that those are all different categories and now, I want to give people the opportunity to learn it in a simpler way.

Nationality is where you hold citizenship. You can be German by nationality but Chinese by ethnicity; this means that someone of Chinese descent was born in Germany or they obtained citizenship in

Germany.

There are even certain countries that allow dual citizenship as well. With dual citizenship, you have the advantages of having the privileges of opportunities to get in both countries but you are also responsible for both of those countries you have citizenship as well.

How do you change your nationality? One common way of how you can change nationalities include marrying someone from another country which is known as the K-1 visa in The United States. Others might go for a work visa or may have been refugees where they can seek asylum in that case.

Race is more broad. Asia is split between the major regions consisting of Central Asia, East Asia, South Asia, Southeast Asia, and West Asia. For example, Uzbekistan is in Central Asia, Mongolia is located in East Asia, while Afghanistan is located in South Asia, Vietnam is in Southeast Asia, and Iran is located in West Asia. Then the Asian part of Russia is considered North Asia. The backgrounds of these people are all different from each country as in culture, language, cuisine, etc. but they still share one similar trait. They are all considered Asian.

Ethnicity is your genetic makeup. Many people are made up of multiple different ethnicities especially here in the United States. Say someone from The United States' biological dad is half Cambodian and half Thai and then their biological mom is fully Japanese, this would make their child a quarter Cambodian, a quarter Thai and half Japanese with having their Nationality as American unless they decide to change it later on.

Out of the three things we discussed in this chapter, we now understand that it is always possible to change one of these, which is nationality. Race along with ethnicity is something you are born with.

Major Religions in Asia

<u>Buddhism</u> - The Buddha is not looked at as a God. He was a man born in Lumbini located in present day Nepal into a life of luxury but once he ran into a dead man, a man with disease and an elderly man, he left his whole life of luxury to get to know about the outside world and later achieve enlightenment. Some practices of the religion include no killing living things, no stealing, no talking bad about someone especially behind their back, no intoxicants and no adultery or having too much sexual pleasure. Their setting of religious practice is a Buddhist temple.

<u>Hinduism</u> - The world's oldest religion that is practiced by 1.2 billion people following it mainly in

India and Nepal. There are over 33 million Hindu Gods/Goddesses but common Gods include Ganesh (God of beginnings), Brahma (God of creation), and Vishnu (known as the protector of the Universe). Common Goddesses include Lakshmi (Goddess of wealth), and Parvati (Goddess of fertility). Common beliefs in Hinduism include karma (when your actions reflect how your future will be), and reincarnation (when your soul is reborn into another body). A hindus place of worship is called a mandir, it is commonly known as a Hindu temple.

Islam - The second largest religion in the world that originated in Saudi Arabia. 20% come from the Arab world. While it started there, the highest Muslim population is located in Indonesia, a country in Southeast Asia. The holy book is called the Quran. Common beliefs in that religion include believing that Muhammad is known to be the final prophet and not to eat pork. The five pillars include believing in only one God (Allah), to pray five times a day, give to charity, to make a pilgrimage to Mecca, the Holy city, at least once in their life and to fast during the month of Ramadan every year. Fasting during Ramadan is suggested for Muslims who are fully capable to mentally and physically. If you are menstruating, pregnant, people who are sick, breastfeeding, the elderly, children who haven't reached puberty, travelers and those in battle then you are exempt from participating. Their place of worship is called a Mosque.

<u>Jainism</u> - A religion that was founded in Eastern India. It has about 4 million followers. Scholars believe this religion was founded around the 7th-5th century BC. Common beliefs in the religion include reincarnation, to not hurt any living thing (this goes for humans, plants, animals, and nature), and to be vegetarian. One of the most influential Jinas was said to be Mahavira. He is the 24th and last Jina.

A Jina is said to be a term that describes "a liberated great teacher." Their place of worship is called a Derasar, also known as a Jain temple.

<u>Sikhism</u> - A religion that has existed since the late 15th century that came from the Punjab region of the Indian subcontinent. The people of this religion are called Sikhs and in this religion many believe in helping out the less fortunate, equality for humans no matter what race or caste they come from and believing in one God called Waheguru. Their place of worship is called a Gurdwara.

<u>Shintoism</u> - A religion that originated in Japan with around 3 million followers. It was said to start in the late 6th century AD. They are a polytheistic religion believing in Kami, sacred spirits that take on other forms. This can be wind, rain, mountains, trees, rivers, fertility, etc. A place of worship is known as a Shinto Shrine.

Asia is Diverse

In conclusion, Asia is very diverse. I've been called "not a real Asian" by non-Asian people because they told me my country of origin is not located in East Asia and because of how "big" my eyes were. From what I have noticed, non-Asian people expected "true Asians" to have an appearance of pale skin, dark colored almond shaped eyes with monolids and dark colored hair. There are many Asians who have those features but you can't invalidate the other Asians with other features as well just because they don't fit your Asian standards.

To non-Asian people, they have categories of what they think is not a real Asian and "All Asians are the same" and honestly, when they say "All Asians are the same" they are more than likely talking about East Asia even though all of the countries in East Asia are completely different themselves, they will think it has similar cultures because they are ignorant who believe too much in the stereotypes that is said about East Asia.

For example, Korea is split between two different countries. There is South Korea and North Korea. South Korea is ruled under a democratic republic while North Korea is under a dictatorship. They were divided in 1945 for the purposes of war and it got pretty complicated since it involved different countries to make them split up.

Asia has a mix of developed and developing countries. Countries like Japan, South Korea, Singapore, Qatar, and Kuwait are developed. This means that most people who live there have decent paying jobs and the economy is more advanced.

We have multiple countries in Asia and if you can't accept every other country located in Asia as

Asia, then you are ignorant and need to realize that there is a load of diversity in Asia. If you happen to tell Asians that they aren't real Asians, those are your incorrect assumptions and they should be changed because it does happen to hurt others.

My Original Title

Originally I was going to title the book "Sick of your Sh!t" because having to explain why you shouldn't be racist was very tiring to me. Then I realized while in the middle of writing this book that there are people in this world who are going to be ignorant but don't exactly know that it is hurtful to other people especially when these people we want to educate are a younger audience. I then decided to name the title Understanding Asian Americans. I wanted this title to be simple yet catch a lot of attention especially to people living in The United States.

I say The US because these issues are mainly where it happened and is happening and I was born and raised in The US so I know the most about what is happening with Asians around me and myself. I can't speak for Asians in Asia or those who are living in different continents but I am open to hearing their experiences as well as I'm curious to know how their experiences were.

The Process of Writing This Book

Hopefully by this time, you are able to understand more of the Asian American perspective on how we feel with racism taking place in this country. This was a book to talk about our experiences and the normalized racism towards Asian Americans as it is not called out as much. I wasn't here to say that Asians are perfect, I understand that there are a lot of problematic things we have done in our community, but not all of us are the same. I was here to point out what you should know is okay to think about Asian people. We are not a model minority like people might think we are, we still go through discrimination and you would know if you ever opened a history book. There are good and bad people in every community so we shouldn't judge someone based on their cultural identity.

Writing my first draft, I honestly went off. It sounded very aggressive. I realized that I needed to tone it down a bit since I want to attract a big audience and some people in this audience are ignorant but it is still possible to have them understand later on. I realized that I didn't want these ignorant people to be ashamed but instead have them learn it was wrong to think that way and there is still time to change your mindset. Some of these people don't mean to be ignorant but it's just how they were raised. Fortunately, we can still change people's minds. Like when we write persuasive essays or a persuasive speech we have the chance to influence people.

I started writing this book during August of 2020 when I entered my Freshman year of college. I finally finished writing right when I entered my Sophomore year of college but still had to work on grammar, fact checking and including more information when needed.

I'm very nervous yet excited to publish this book. It's my first book that I put a lot of time and effort into and I can't wait for people to read it and I hope they learn something new from this. I know I did.

I have multiple reasons why I wrote a book like this but the main reason why was because as a person of color, I am tired of racism I will forever have to face. Even back in history many still have the trauma their ancestors went through.

Racism is everywhere, some parts aren't as bad compared to others. In The United States I would say the level of racism is prevalent, especially in the South. I've heard literal horror stories from people who lived there and from what you see on the news.

As of right now, I have decided to have two more books to complete this series but I won't work on them until after 2025. In the meantime, I would like to focus on making fiction books. I like to write fiction because when writing in that section there are no limitations with what you want to have happen in your book.

During my writing journey, I had planned for my first book to be a fictional book but I then came in contact with a lot of writer's block and started writing this book in the middle of writing the fictional book. I realized that since I'm more passionate about writing about this that I should focus on this one first. I wanted my readers to get to know me, especially about my identity. I know I am not the only one who has dealt with the situations I've been in and hopefully there is going to be change because it should not be like that.

I'm really glad that I had the opportunity to write this and publish this at the right time. I started creating projects for future stories I should write when I was around sixteen and didn't think about publishing until I was around twenty-five because I wanted to focus on school but realized that I can manage my time with both.

Acknowledgements

Someone I would like to thank for helping me with this project is my best friend, Yzabella Estacio. She has inspired me to want to write this book, inspired me to start my writing journey earlier in my life and has designed this amazing cover photo.

REFERENCES

"8 Things That India Gifted The World & Are Still In Use!" The StoryPedia, http://www.thestorypedia.com/entertainment/bet-not-know-8-invented-india/.

"9 Facts You Might Not Know About The Sari — Google Arts & Culture." Google Arts & Culture, Google Arts & Culture, https://artsandculture.google.com/story/9-facts-you-might-not-know-about-the-sari/ewIi5LK9aiamJA.

"10 Hindu Gods and Goddesses You Need to Know." Blue Osa Yoga Retreat + Spa, 25 Nov. 2014, https://www.blueosa.com/10-hindu-deities-every-one-know-pilgrimage-india/.

"14 Frequently Asked Questions - Hinduism Today." Hinduism Today, 6 Feb. 2020, https://www.hinduismtoday.com/modules/smartsection/item.php?itemid=5666.

"20 Clever Inventions You Probably Didn't Know Were Made By Indians." Storypick, https://www.storypick.com/20-clever-inventions-probably-did-nt-know-made-indians/.

"A Brief History of the Qipao: China's Sexiest Dress - SupChina." SupChina,

https://signal.supchina.com/a-brief-history-of-the-qipao-chinas-sexiest-dress/.

"About Sikhism ." Mesaaz , https://www.mesaaz.gov/home/showpublisheddocu-

ment/22622/636358835451330000#:~:text=Sikhism%20is%20the%20world's%20

fifth,monotheistic%20religion%20in%20the%20world%20.&text=Sikhs%20

believes%20in%20one%20omnipresent,Wa%2DHEY%2Dguru).

"A Cultural History of White Girls Wearing Bindis." VICE - VICE Is the Defin-

itive Guide to Enlightening Information., 5700553057239040, https://www.vice.

com/en/article/xye97d/a-cultural-history-of-white-girls-wearing-bindis.

Adhikari, Saugat. "Top 10 Hindu Goddesses - Ancient History Lists." Ancient

History Lists, 1 Dec. 2016, https://www.ancienthistorylists.com/india-history/

top-10-hindu-goddesses/.

Akiko. "Is The Word J*p Derogatory? ." Japan-Talk, 5 May 2014, https://www.

japan-talk.com/jt/new/is-the-word-J*p-derogatory.

"Altaic of China." Encyclopædia Britannica, Encyclopædia Britannica, 30 Nov. 2021, https://www.britannica.com/place/China/Altaic.

Amendral, Aurora. "How The Pandemic Has Upended The Lives Of Thailand's Sex Workers." Npr, 3 Feb. 2021, https://www.npr.org/sections/goatsandsoda/2021/02/03/960848011/how-the-pandemic-has-upended-the-lives-of-thailands-sex-workers.

Andrews, Jessica. "We Interviewed 5 Cultural Appropriators at Coachella 2018 | Teen Vogue." Teen Vogue, Teen Vogue, 20 Apr. 2018, https://www.teenvogue.com/story/cultural-appropriation-coachella-2018.

"A New Community | Chinese | Immigration and Relocation in U.S. History | Classroom Materials at the Library of Congress | Library of Congress." The Library of Congress, https://www.loc.gov/classroom-materials/immigration/chinese/a-new-community/.

"Bahasa Indonesian | Asia Society." Asia Society, https://asiasociety.org/education/bahasa-indonesian.

"BBC - Religions - Hinduism: Lakshmi." BBC - Home, https://www.bbc.co.uk/religion/religions/hinduism/deities/lakshmi.shtml.

"BBC - Religions - Hinduism: Vishnu." BBC - Home, https://www.bbc.co.uk/religion/religions/hinduism/deities/vishnu.shtml#:~:text=Vishnu%20is%20the%20preserver%20and,balance%20of%20good%20and%20evil.&text=Vishnu's%20worshippers%2C%20usually%20called%20Vaishnava%2C%20consider%20him%20the%20greatest%20god.

"BBC - Religions - Jainism: Jain Temples." BBC - Home, https://www.bbc.co.uk/religion/religions/jainism/worship/temples_1.shtml.

Belludi, Nagesh. "Was the Buddha a God or a Superhuman? - Right Attitudes." Right Attitudes, 1 June 2015, https://www.rightattitudes.com/2015/06/01/was-the-buddha-god-or-superhuman.

"British Library." The British Library - The British Library, https://www.bl.uk/onlinegallery/features/sacred/wfabelief.html.

"Brunei ." Nationsonline, https://www.nationsonline.org/oneworld/brunei.htm.

"Buddhist Countries 2021." 2021 World Population by Country, https://worldpopulationreview.com/country-rankings/buddhist-countries.

"Catholicism in the Philippines during the Spanish Colonial Period 1521-1898 | 4 Corners of the World: International Collections and Studies at the Library of Congress." Library of Congress Blogs, https://blogs.loc.gov/international-collections/2018/07/catholicism-in-the-philippines-during-the-spanish-colonial-period-1521-1898/#:~:text=The%20first%20recorded%20conversion%20in,up%20to%20eight%20hundred%20Cebuanos.

Chan, Justin. "Rapper Slammed for Appropriating Asian Culture: '[This] Is Not Your Aesthetic.'" Yahoo | Mail, Weather, Search, Politics, News, Finance, Sports & Videos, Yahoo, 30 July 2020, https://www.yahoo.com/now/rapper-slammed-appropriating-asian-culture-210254115.html.

"Chinese Exclusion Act." HISTORY, A&E Television Networks, 17 Mar. 2021, https://www.history.com/topics/immigration/chinese-exclusion-act-1882.

Chow, Kat. "If We Called Ourselves Yellow ." Npr.Org, 27 Sept. 2018,

https://www.npr.org/sections/codeswitch/2018/09/27/647989652/if-we-

called-ourselves-yellow.

"Civil Liberties Act of 1988." Encyclopedia.Densho.Org/, https://encyclopedia.

densho.org/Civil_Liberties_Act_of_1988/.

"Countries Allowing Dual Citizenship USA | NNU Immigration." NNU

Immigration, 1 July 2021, https://www.nnuimmigration.com/dual-citizen-

ship-usa/#:~:text=Dual%20citizenship%20refers%20to%20the,each%20

of%20the%20two%20nations.

De Leon, Kayla. "How Filipinos Were Forced To Change Their Surnames: The

Catálogo Alfab – Narra Studio." Narra Studio, Narra Studio, 12 July 2020,

https://narrastudio.com/blogs/journal/remnants-of-our-colonized-names#:~:-

text=The%20pre%2Dcolonial%20Filipino%20identity,to%20make%20

the%20census%20easier.

Dhir, Rajeev. "Tugrik (MNT) Definition." Investopedia, Investopedia, 29 Jan.

2010, https://www.investopedia.com/terms/t/tugrik.asp.

"Discover Cambodia's French Colonial Architecture." Book with Confidence |

Enchanting Travels: Luxury Private Tours, Enchanting Travels, 19 May 2019,

https://www.enchantingtravels.com/travel-blog/discover-cambodias-french-co-

lonial-architecture/.

Farha, Fatima. "Why 'Bindis' Should Not Be a Fashion Trend – Niles West

News." Niles West News, https://nileswestnews.org/31336/west-word/

bindis-are-not-a-fashion-trend/.

"Forms of Privilege | MediaSmarts." MediaSmarts, 21 Feb. 2012, https://

mediasmarts.ca/diversity-media/privilege-media/forms-privilege.

"Ganesha." Encyclopædia Britannica, Encyclopædia Britannica,

https://www.britannica.com/topic/Ganesha.

"G**k Definition & Meaning | Dictionary.Com." Www.Dictionary.Com, https://

www.dictionary.com/browse/g**k.

Goswami, Avani. "The Beautiful History & Culture Behind Bindi - Jetset Times."

Jetset Times, Jetset Times, 17 Sept. 2020, https://jetsettimes.com/countries/india/

the-history-culture-behind-bindi/.

"Gurdwara." Encyclopædia Britannica, Encyclopædia Britannica, https://www.

britannica.com/topic/gurdwara.

Gutierrez, Elizabeth. "THE -DOTBUSTER- ATTACKS: HATE CRIME

AGAINST ASIAN INDIANS IN JERSEY CITY, NEW JERSEY ."

Citeseerx.Ist.Psu.Edu/, https://citeseerx.ist.psu.edu/viewdoc/download?-

doi=10.1.1.572.2245&rep=rep1&type=pdf.

Hayes, Marques. "What Languages Are Spoken In Mongolia? - WorldAtlas."

WorldAtlas, WorldAtlas, 8 Sept. 2017, https://www.worldatlas.com/articles/

what-languages-are-spoken-in-mongolia.html.

Hays, Jeffrey. "LANGUAGES IN KAZAKHSTAN | Facts and Details." Facts

and Details, http://factsanddetails.com/central-asia/Kazakhstan/sub8_4b/

entry-4636.html.

"Hinduism: Sacred Spaces and Places | URI." Homepage | URI, https://www.uri.org/kids/world-religions/hindu-spaces.

"History of Candles - Who Invented Candle?" History of Lighting - Development of Lighting Technology, http://www.historyoflighting.net/lighting-history/history-of-candles/.

History.com Editors. "Buddhism." HISTORY, A&E Television Networks, 15 Sept. 2021, https://www.history.com/topics/religion/buddhism.

"Hollywood Actress Dubbed 'Godmother of Vietnamese Nail Industry.'" Abc7.Com, https://abc7.com/vietnamese-nail-salon-nails-vietnam/688205/.

"Islam." HISTORY, A&E Television Networks, 18 Nov. 2021, https://www.history.com/topics/religion/islam.

"Japanese Internment Camps." HISTORY, A&E Television Networks, 18 Nov. 2021, https://www.history.com/topics/world-war-ii/japanese-american-relocation.

"How India Gave 'Shampoo' To The World, Thanks to Sake Dean Mahomed." The Better India, https://www.thebetterindia.com/180211/india-gift-shampoo-world-sake-dean-mohamed-london-history/.

"How Korea's 'Nones' Differ from Religiously Unaffiliated Americans | Center for Religion and Civic Culture." Center for Religion and Civic Culture, https://crcc.usc.edu/how-korean-religious-nones-differ-from-unaffiliated-americans/.

Hsu, Leina. "The Dark Side Of Sex Tourism In Asia - Women's Republic." Women's Republic, Women's Republic, 22 July 2020, https://www.womensrepublic.net/the-dark-side-of-sex-tourism-in-asia/#:~:text=Asia's%20Market%20for%20Sex,to%2014%20percent%20of%20GDP.

"Introduction - Chinese Exclusion Act: Primary Documents in American History - Research Guides at Library of Congress." Home - Research Guides at Library of Congress, https://guides.loc.gov/chinese-exclusion-act.

"Issei and Nisei: Definition & WW2 - Video & Lesson Transcript | Study.Com."

Study.Com, https://study.com/academy/lesson/issei-and-nisei-definition-ww2.html.

Jaen, Rej. "Top Religions in Asia | Breaking Asia." Breaking Asia | Explore

the Infinite Far East, 29 Dec. 2018, https://www.breakingasia.com/culture/

top-religions-in-asia/.

"Jainism." Encyclopædia Britannica, Encyclopædia Britannica, https://www.

britannica.com/topic/Jainism.

"Jainism | National Geographic Society." National Geographic Society, 14 Sept.

2020, https://www.nationalgeographic.org/encyclopedia/jainism/.

"Japanese American Internment." Encyclopædia Britannica, Encyclopædia Britanni-

ca, 18 Oct. 2021, https://www.britannica.com/event/Japanese-American-internment.

"Japanese-American Internment During World War II | National Archives."

National Archives, 15 Aug. 2016, https://www.archives.gov/education/

lessons/japanese-relocation.

Kaur, Harmeet. "Here's Why Sikhs Were Offended by This $790 Gucci Turban - CNN Style." CNN, CNN, 19 May 2019, https://www.cnn.com/style/article/gucci-turban-sikh-trnd/index.html.

"Kimono and Kimono Rental Services in Japan." Japan-Guide.Com - Japan Travel and Living Guide, https://www.japan-guide.com/e/e2101.html#:~:text=The%20kimono%20(%E7%9D%80%E7%89%A9)%20is%20a,formal%20traditional%20events%20and%20funerals.&text=The%20outfit%20is%20accompanied%20-by,a%20small%20handbag%20for%20women.

Kiprop, Joseph. "What Language Is Spoken in Palestine? - WorldAtlas." WorldAtlas, WorldAtlas, 10 Oct. 2018, https://www.worldatlas.com/articles/what-language-is-spoken-in-palestine.html.

"Life in the Camps." Encyclopædia Britannica, Encyclopædia Britannica, https://www.britannica.com/event/Japanese-American-internment/Life-in-the-camps.

"List of Asian Capitals by Countries." Countries of the World: Flags, Capitals, Currencies, Time Zones, Calling Codes, TLDs, https://www.countries-ofthe-world.com/capitals-of-asia.html.

"List of Asian Currencies By Countries Updated 2021." Flags of The World | Flags

Images, Meaning, History, https://flagsworld.org/currencies-asia.html.

"List of Asian Countries with Asian Languages, Nationalities & Flags • 7ESL."

7ESL, https://7esl.com/asian-countries-languages-flags/.

Lum, Jessica. "Racist Video Rant about Asians in UCLA Library Goes Viral |

Hyphen Magazine." Hyphen Magazine, 14 Mar. 2011, https://hyphenmagazine.

com/blog/2011/03/racist-video-rant-about-asians-ucla-library-goes-viral.

"Lumbini, the Birthplace of the Lord Buddha - UNESCO World Heritage Centre."

UNESCO World Heritage Centre, https://whc.unesco.org/en/list/666/.

"Malay (Bahasa Melayu) Language - Structure, Writing & Alphabet - MustGo."

MustGo.Com, https://www.mustgo.com/worldlanguages/bahasa-melayu-malay/.

Mark, Joshua J. "Buddhism - World History Encyclopedia." World History

Encyclopedia, World History Encyclopedia, 25 Sept. 2020, https://www.ancient.eu/

buddhism/#:~:text=Buddhism%20is%20a%20non%2Dtheistic,the%20Buddha%20

l.%20c.%20563%20%2D%20c.

"Marvel Star Slates 'racist' Hollywood over Name Change - BBC News." BBC News, BBC News, 31 Aug. 2017, https://www.bbc.com/news/entertainment-arts-41107089.

"Middle East Facts | Idaho State University." Idaho State University, https://www.isu.edu/history/student-opportunities/class-projects/middle-east-facts/.

"Milestones: 1866–1898 - Office of the Historian." Office of the Historian, https://history.state.gov/milestones/1866-1898/chinese-immigration.

"Milestones: 1937–1945 - Office of the Historian." Office of the Historian, https://history.state.gov/milestones/1937-1945/chinese-exclusion-act-repeal#:~:text=In%201943%2C%20Congress%20passed%20a,around%20105%20visas%20per%20year.

"MTV News - The Weird History of Asian Sex Stereotypes." Facebook Watch, MTV News, 25 May 2016, https://www.facebook.com/mtvnews/videos/1153358331373016/.

"Muslim Population by Country 2021." 2021 World Population by Country, https://worldpopulationreview.com/country-rankings/muslim-population-by-country.

Nag, Oishimaya Sen. "What Languages Are Spoken in Brunei? - WorldAtlas." WorldAtlas, WorldAtlas, 1 July 2017, https://www.worldatlas.com/articles/what-languages-are-spoken-in-brunei.html.

"Native North Americans - The Effects of Colonization." Chino.K12.ca.Us/, https://www.chino.k12.ca.us/cms/lib8/CA01902308/Centricity/domain/2247/unit%202/Native%20North%20Americans.doc%20unit%202.pdf.

"National Language of India: With Official & Minority Language." Career Power: Prepare for Bank, SSC, Railway, UPSC, JEE-NEET & Teaching Exams, https://www.careerpower.in/national-language-of-india.html.

"Nextshark." Instagram, https://www.instagram.com/p/B-nWQrngOQc/.

"Nextshark ." Instagram, https://www.instagram.com/p/B-nbuyige03/.

O'Brien, Barbara. "Who Was the Buddha, and What Did He Teach? - Lion's Roar."

Lion's Roar, https://www.lionsroar.com/who-was-the-buddha/.

"Official and Spoken Languages of Countries in Asia and the Middle East. ."

Nationsonline, https://www.nationsonline.org/oneworld/asian_languages.htm.

"On May 06, 1882: Chinese Exclusion Act Signed into Law." Home | A History of

Racial Injustice, https://calendar.eji.org/racial-injustice/may/6.

"Our Documents - Chinese Exclusion Act (1882)." Welcome to OurDocuments.Gov,

https://www.ourdocuments.gov/doc.php?flash=false&doc=47.

Pariona, Amber. "Countries That Are Most And Least Proficient In English -

WorldAtlas." WorldAtlas, WorldAtlas, 14 June 2017, https://www.worldatlas.com/

articles/countries-that-are-most-and-least-proficient-in-english.html.

Perkins, McKenzie. "East Timor Religion." Learn Religions, Learn Religions, 13

Aug. 2019, https://www.learnreligions.com/east-timor-religion-4766639.

"P*ki Definition & Meaning - Merriam-Webster." Dictionary by Merriam-Webster: America's Most-Trusted Online Dictionary, https://www.merriam-webster.com/dictionary/P*ki.

"Palestine." HISTORY, A&E Television Networks, 12 Nov. 2021, https://www.history.com/topics/middle-east/palestine#:~:text=Today%2C%20Arab%20people%20who%20call,contested%20region%20of%20the%20world.

"Political Impact Of Colonial Powers Upon Southeast Asia History Essay." UK Essays | UKEssays, UK Essays, 12 Aug. 2021, https://www.ukessays.com/essays/history/political-impact-of-colonial-powers-upon-southeast-asia-history-essay.php.

"Qing Dynasty." HISTORY, A&E Television Networks, 21 Aug. 2018, https://www.history.com/topics/china/qing-dynasty#:~:text=The%20Qing%20Dynasty%20was%20the,ruled%20by%20the%20Han%20people.

"Ramadan The Practice of Fasting." Eatright.Org - Academy of Nutrition and Dietetics, https://www.eatright.org/health/lifestyle/culture-and-traditions/ramadan--the-practice-of-fasting#:~:text=As%20one%20of%20the%20five,mothers%20and%20travelers%20are%20exempt.

"RELIGION IN JAPAN AND THE IRRELIGIOUS JAPANESE | Facts and Details." Facts and Details, https://factsanddetails.com/japan/cat16/sub182/item592.html.

"Religion in the Philippines | Asia Society." Asia Society, https://asiasociety.org/education/religion-philippines#:~:text=Spain%20introduced%20Christianity%20to%20the,Indonesia%20into%20the%20Philippine%20archipelago.

"Religions in Vietnam – Travel Information for Vietnam from Local Experts." Travel Information for Vietnam from Local Experts, https://www.vietnamvisa-easy.com/blog/religions-in-vietnam/.

"Religion of Malaysia." Encyclopædia Britannica, Encyclopædia Britannica, https://www.britannica.com/place/Malaysia/Religion.

"Religion of Russia." Encyclopædia Britannica, Encyclopædia Britannica, 1 Jan. 2022, https://www.britannica.com/place/Russia/Religion.

"Resolution Opposing Use of Racial Slurs in Business Names."
Philadelphiabar.Org/, https://www.philadelphiabar.org/page/ResolutionOppos-
ingRacialSlurs?appNum=2.

"Russian Language - Structure, Writing & Alphabet - MustGo." MustGo.Com,
https://www.mustgo.com/worldlanguages/russian/.

"Sex Tourism in Thailand: What Where and Why - Tourism Teacher." Tourism
Teacher, 23 Sept. 2019, https://tourismteacher.com/sex-tourism-in-thailand-
what-where-and-why/.

Shawish, Hesham. "Campaign to Save the Arabic Language in Lebanon - BBC
News." Bbc.Com/, BBC News, 24 June 2010, https://www.bbc.com/news/10316914.

"Shinto." Japan-Guide.Com - Japan Travel and Living Guide, https://www.
japan-guide.com/e/e2056.html.

"Shinto | University of St Andrews." University of St Andrews - Scotland's First University, Founded 1413, https://www.st-andrews.ac.uk/hr/edi/religionbelief/shinto/#:~:text=Worldwide%20followers%20(Estimated)%3A%203,shrine%20dedicated%20to%20the%20Kami.

"Shintoism." Website for Queensborough Community College, https://www.qcc.cuny.edu/socialsciences/ppecorino/phil_of_religion_text/chapter_2_religions/Shintoism.htm#:~:text=In%20the%20late%206th%20century,a%20previous%20state%20of%20existence.

"Sikhism." Encyclopædia Britannica, Encyclopædia Britannica, https://www.britannica.com/topic/Sikhism.

"South Korea Religions - Demographics." IndexMundi - Country Facts, https://www.indexmundi.com/south_korea/religions.html.

"South Korean Culture - Religion — Cultural Atlas." Cultural Atlas, https://culturalatlas.sbs.com.au/south-korean-culture/south-korean-culture-religion.

"Spanish Influence in the Philippines – Lifey." Lifey, http://lifey.org/spanish-in-fluence-on-the-philippines/.

Staff. "Why Do Sikh Men Wear Turbans? - CSMonitor.Com." The Christian Science Monitor, The Christian Science Monitor, 6 Aug. 2012, https://www.csmonitor.com/World/Asia-South-Central/2012/0806/5-things-to-know-about-Sikhism/Why-do-Sikh-men-wear-turbans.

"#StopAsianHate - Fight Anti-Asian Racism." STOPASIANHATE.INFO, https://www.stopasianhate.info/.

Szczepanski, Kallie. "Kites, Maps, Glass and Other Asian Inventions." ThoughtCo, ThoughtCo, 20 June 2008, https://www.thoughtco.com/ancient-asian-inventions-195169.

"Taiwan." Nationsonline, https://www.nationsonline.org/oneworld/taiwan.htm.

"The Chinese Exclusion Act Ended Seventy-One Years Ago, Today." NBC News, 17 Dec. 2014, https://www.nbcnews.com/news/asian-america/chinese-exclusion-act-ended-seventy-one-years-ago-today-n270276.

"The Choice of Nationality." https://www.moj.go.jp/ENGLISH/
information/tcon-01.html.

https://www.moj.go.jp/ENGLISH/information/tcon-01.html.

"The Evolution of Shanghai Fashion « Historic Shanghai." Historic Shanghai,
https://www.historic-shanghai.com/the-evolution-of-shanghai-fashion/.

"The Five Pillars of Islam." Metmuseum.Org, https://www.metmuseum.
org/learn/educators/curriculum-resources/art-of-the-islamic-world/unit-one/
the-five-pillars-of-islam.

"The Five Precepts - Buddhist Beliefs - Edexcel - GCSE Religious Studies
Revision - Edexcel - BBC Bitesize." BBC Bitesize, https://www.bbc.co.uk/
bitesize/guides/zf8g4qt/revision/9.

The Infographics Show. Why Did Korea Split in to North and South? YouTube, 10
Oct. 2018, https://www.youtube.com/watch?v=BBPwM1Takwg.

"The Practice | The Model Minority Myth." The Practice, https://thepractice.law.

harvard.edu/article/the-model-minority-myth/.

"The Secret Lives of Sex Tourists - World Travel Guide." World Travel Guide,

http://wtgtravelguide, https://www.worldtravelguide.net/features/feature/

the-secret-lives-of-sex-tourists/.

"To All The Boys I've Loved Before Actor Put on Blast for Racially-Insensitive

Tweets - FASHION Magazine." FASHION Magazine, 22 Aug. 2018, https://fash-

ionmagazine.com/flare/celebrity/to-all-the-boys-ive-loved-before-racist-tweets/.

"Top 20 Ancient Chinese Inventions." China.Usc.Edu, https://china.usc.edu/sites/

default/files/forums/Chinese%20Inventions.pdf.

"Top 20 Family Names in the Philippines." Tagaloglang.Com, https://www.

tagaloglang.com/most-common-filipino-surnames/.

"Understanding Shinto - Japan's Ancient Religion - Japanology." Japanology, 9 May

2018, https://japanology.org/2018/05/understanding-shinto-japans-ancient-religion/.

Victorian, Brande. "24 Famous Women Of Proud African And Asian Heritage
- Essence." Essence, Essence, 4 Mar. 2021, https://www.essence.com/celebrity/
famous-women-of-african-and-asian-heritage/#1042895.

Vox. "Yellowface Is a Bad Look, Hollywood." Youtube.Com, YouTube, 21 Apr.
2016, https://www.youtube.com/watch?v=zB0lrSebyng.

Wanjek, Christopher. "The Great Shampoo Sham | Live Science." Livescience.
Com, Live Science, 9 June 2009, https://www.livescience.com/3659-great-
shampoo-sham.html.

---. "Racial Slurs (C**nk)." Northwest Asian Weekly, 1 Sept. 2011, http://
nwasianweekly.com/2011/09/racial-slurs-c**nk/.

"What Is a Qipao? Discover The History Of This Gorgeous Garment." LTL
Shanghai, 6 Dec. 2018, https://www.ltl-shanghai.com/qipao/.

"What Is Jina? - Definition from Yogapedia." Yogapedia.Com, https://www.
yogapedia.com/definition/11172/jina.

"What Are The Five Regions of Asia? - WorldAtlas." WorldAtlas, WorldAtlas, 10 Feb. 2018, https://www.worldatlas.com/articles/the-four-regions-of-asia.html.

"What to Wear When Visiting a Mosque - Tourism Teacher." Tourism Teacher, 19 Sept. 2019, https://tourismteacher.com/what-to-wear-when-visiting-a-mosque/.

"World Religions." InfoPlease, https://www.infoplease.com/world/social-statistics/world-religions.

Wuh, Rayna. "Opinion | Racist Fetishization Underlays Atlanta Shooting - The Daily Illini." The Daily Illini, https://dailyillini.com/opinions-stories/2021/04/01/opinion-racist-fetishization-underlays-atlanta-shooting/.

"Xenophobia: Definiton, Pronunciation, Examples, and More." Healthline, Healthline Media, 27 July 2021, https://www.healthline.com/health/xenophobia#signs-and-symptoms.

Zhu, Michelle. "All the Times People Have Called Me 'C**nk' to My Face." VICE - VICE Is the Definitive Guide to Enlightening Information., 5700553057239040, https://www.vice.com/en/article/gyjgvx/all-the-times-white-people-have-called-me-c**nk-to-my-face.